GUIDE
to Selecting
and Acquiring
CD-ROMs, SOFTWARE, AND OTHER ELECTRONIC PUBLICATIONS

Stephen Bosch
Patricia Promis
Chris Sugnet

PUBLICATIONS COMMITTEE
OF THE ACQUISITION OF
LIBRARY MATERIALS SECTION
ASSOCIATION FOR LIBRARY
COLLECTIONS & TECHNICAL
SERVICES

American Library Association
Chicago and London 1994

Cover design by Donavan Vicha

Interior design by Harriett Banner

Composition by ALA Books/Production Services, in Times Roman and Helvetica using Ventura Publisher 3.0 and camera-ready pages output on a Varityper VT600 laser printer

Printed on 50-pound Finch Opaque, a pH-neutral stock, and bound in 90-pound Scott Index by IPC, St. Joseph, Michigan

The paper used in this publication meets the minimum requirements of American National Standard for Information Sciences—Permanence of Paper for Printed Library Materials, ANSI Z39.48-1984. ∞

Library of Congress Cataloging-in-Publication Data
Bosch, Stephen.
    Guide to selecting and acquiring CD-ROMs, software, and other
electronic publications / Stephen Bosch, Patricia Promis, Chris Sugnet.
        p.   cm.—(Acquisition guidelines ; no. 9)
    Includes index.
    ISBN 0-8389-0629-X
    1. Acquisition of data bases—United States. 2. Acquisition of
computer programs—United States.   3. Acquisition of video
recordings—United States. I. Promis, Patricia.   II. Sugnet, Chris
L. III. Title. IV. Series.
Z689.A2746   1973 no. 9
[Z692.D38]
025.2 s—dc20   93-43298
[025.2'84]   CIP

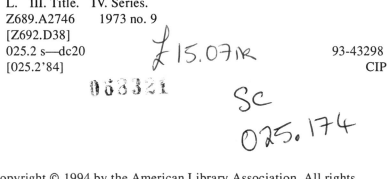

Printed in the United States of America.

98 97 96 95   5 4 3

Contents

I. Introduction

The acquisition of electronic formats for library collections is a complex process. Many factors are involved with purchasing electronic formats including such variables as choice of format, vendor, etc.; the necessary purchase of computer hardware; preservation concerns; and the growing need of libraries to offer access to information in several formats. The pressure on libraries to offer new services, new materials, and new electronic formats to their clientele is continuously growing, as is the escalating cost of these materials. Since budgetary constraints currently facing libraries will continue into the foreseeable future, it is necessary for libraries to carefully assess and execute purchases of information in electronic format.

A. Purpose of This *Guide*

The purpose of this *Guide* is to provide directions and suggestions for acquiring collections of electronic library materials. It does not cover remote access via telecommunication to commercial or Internet information sources. The intent is to delineate the steps involved in the process of purchasing electronic materials. Acquiring these products requires an entirely new set of considerations not previously used when selecting and purchasing material in more traditional formats. Unlike printed information, accessing electronically formatted information requires additional tools such as a machine (computer/hardware) and a special program (software). Purchasing hardware and software also entails working with new vendors who may not be familiar with library needs and methods of doing business.

B. Definitions of Materials Discussed

Materials in electronic format discussed in this *Guide* include resources that are optically and magnetically stored and retrieved through the use of electronic technology and made available as individual products. This information can be stored in either a digital or an analog format. Some of this information can be manipulated through the use of computers, and because of this unique characteristic, interaction between the end user and the information product becomes an important consideration in purchasing.

Examples of information in electronic format include:

1. Full text files, such as encyclopedias, patents, directories, journals, etc.
2. Numeric data files, such as census, stock market, or the Social Science Data tapes from I.C.P.S.R. (Inter-University Consortium for Political and Social Research)
3. Indexes to current journal literature stored on CD-ROMs or a computer hard disk
4. Software, computer programs, and non-numeric machine readable data files
5. Videotapes, videodiscs, and videogames.

C. Scope

This *Guide* covers most of the existing electronic formats available for libraries of all types. It is important to note from the outset that this document is written primarily for libraries that are educational in mission. With the possible exception of corporate libraries, most items discussed will be of value to all libraries. (Corporate libraries do not fall under all the copyright guidelines governed by the fair use doctrine for educational purposes; therefore some issues concerning copyrights, licenses, and lease agreements may not be applicable.) This *Guide* provides information pertinent to the selection and acquisitions process and addresses various issues connected with copyright concerns, licensing considerations, the need for developing appropriate standards, prices, establishing LANs, etc. A glossary of terms most commonly used in the library world when referring to these materials is included. There is also a list of sources that can be consulted for more detailed information.

II. Discussion of Material Types

Material types are evolving rapidly because of changes in technology. The acquiring of information in electronic format involves consistent monitoring of the professional literature for changes in technology. The following material types are the most widely available formats as of fall 1993.

A. CD-ROM (does not include music CDs)

CD-ROM is the acronym for *compact disc-read only memory*. This technology relies upon the use of a beam of light (laser) to reflect off patterns embedded in a polycarbonate disc. The reflected beam of light is then "read" by the machine and turned into information or images. The standard 4.75-inch CD-ROM disc can contain up to 540 megabytes of computer-accessible information. The large 8- or 12-inch video discs can contain up to one gigabyte of computer-accessible information. In addition to computer-accessible information, this technology can encode moving video images, still-frame graphics, and digital and analog audio. These formats can also be combined on a single disc to produce full multimedia applications. CD-ROM technology requires the use of a computer and a special CD-ROM drive to access the information on the actual disc. Currently, most CD-ROM applications use small computers such as the IBM PS series, IBM clones, Apples, Macintoshs, Next workstations, or similar personal computers. These computers are equipped with special interface cards that connect them to the actual CD-ROM drive or player. The CD players used with small computers are different from those sold to play audio compact discs. The controller cards are installed internally in the computer and are accompanied by special software (drivers) that controls the use of the drive. These controller cards vary in cost and capability. Some can handle only one CD-ROM drive at a time, others can handle multiple drives simultaneously. Some computers can be purchased with CD-ROM drives pre-installed (internal) in the system.

There are a wide variety of external CD-ROM drives available. These also vary from units that can read one disc at a time to units that can contain and access multiple discs. Before purchasing a product in CD-ROM format it will be necessary to have clearly defined the hardware needs for the product selected.

In addition to the necessary hardware, software is required to make the information encoded in the CD-ROM disc retrievable. Some products include the software as an integral part of the package. Some products require the purchase and installation of additional software. It is a good idea to investigate packages that combine hardware and software in a single purchase (bundled) to save on costs.

A wide variety of CD-ROM products are available in the marketplace. Consequently, there is going to be a wide variety in the approaches taken to purchase these items. CD-ROMs can be purchased directly from the producer, or from a vendor or network. There are advantages and disadvantages to working with a second party to purchase CD-ROM products. Often, the acquisition of these items is governed by leases and license agreements with the publishers. If it seems necessary to ask for the modification or clarification of these agreements, it may be easier to deal directly with the publisher. A publisher may offer discounts on the purchase of several products, including multiple formats such as paper, CD-ROM, tape. etc., which may not be available from vendors. On the other hand, vendors can offer a valuable service in that they are organized to expedite the ordering, shipping, and invoicing. If several titles from different publishers are to be purchased, it would be more efficient to use a vendor than to contact each publisher individually.

It is possible that the same product is available from different publishers at different prices. Such situations can become complicated as the value added by one publisher may be a searching mode that makes the information much easier to use. Pricing may also be affected by local ownership of print versions of a CD-ROM product. A discounted price may be based on owning the print version and the real cost could escalate if the print version is canceled.

Hardware will also be an issue. When ordering the item it is necessary to clearly state on the purchase order which version (IBM, Apple, etc.) is required, and the disk compatibility (e.g., 5.25- or 3.5-inch, double or high density) for accompanying software. When selecting a CD-ROM it is necessary to carefully analyze system requirements to determine the type of hardware needed. For an in-depth discussion of CD-ROM technology for libraries, consult William Saffady's "CD-ROM: A Survey of Technology, Products, and Applications" (see Sources for Further Information).

B. Videotapes and Videodiscs

Commercial interests have greatly simplified the videotape and video-disc market. A few years ago there were several formats to consider, each requiring different hardware. The VHS format has now become standard in the commercial and educational markets. Videotapes and discs both require the use of a video player or videocassette recorder (VCR) and a video monitor (TV) to display the images produced by the player. Videodiscs utilize the same technology as CD-ROMs for production and retrieval, but do not require a computer interface to display the images. Standard educational, public service, and commercially produced videotapes and discs are available from a wide variety of vendors including some currently used by acquisitions departments for book purchases. Not all materials will be available from vendors and it will be necessary to order some titles directly from the publishers. The acquisition of these materials differs little from that of printed materials, including prices. Specialized academic or educational videos may be much more expensive than those produced for a commercial market. When first released, popular commercial titles will be relatively expensive, ranging from $50 to $100. Unlike books, prices fall dramatically as the market becomes saturated. The prices and services offered by vendors will vary, and it pays to compare them. There is a limited "used" trade but is normally isolated and is not well organized at this time. The purchase of used videotapes as a regular approach to collection development is not recommended for circulating collections.

More and more frequently, libraries are confronted by gifts of home recordings of commercially produced materials. As a rule, the copyright laws do not allow public use of materials recorded for private use. These gifts should not be accepted. Gifts of home videos, those produced privately, can be accepted based on the stated needs of the library's collection development policy.

C. Video Games (instructional and recreational)

The library market is a secondary market for these items, and consequently it must conform to market forces dominated by commercial interests for both educational and recreational video games. In general, this category of materials is characterized by a variety of software cartridges in several formats that generally are designed to operate on one video game system only. Cartridges that run on Nintendo game machines can not be used on other systems and vice versa. Hardware for these items includes the video machine that handles these discs, the controllers (joysticks, etc.), and a video monitor. Some sophisticated games interact with video images from videodiscs or CD-ROMs and may require their use. Some so-called video games are actually computer software and should be treated as software, not as game cartridges that are fitted into particular video game machines. Popular video games are available from the same vendors that handle videotapes, or software, but it may be cost-effective to contact vendors, or mail-order houses that specialize in computer software for these materials.

The commercial video game market has been dominated by proprietary concerns. Until recently, the leading manufacturer used a system design that forced the publishers of game cartridges to incorporate a design of the equipment manufacturers into their game cartridges for use in the system. The result was that games for one system only work on one system. When purchasing items one should be careful to check what systems can use the cartridge.

Video game technology is rapidly evolving. The graphics and details available in a particular application or game have greatly improved as the cost of basic computer chips has come down. As this technology improves, public pressure will force libraries to update their game collections with cartridges for new game machines. The old games won't play on the new machines and before long the current collection of video games may become obsolete.

D. Bibliographic and Full Text Databases: Cost Is Key

During the past few years, storage capacity of computer systems has grown enormously. It is now feasible to consider the purchase of some databases that previously were inconceivable to own and use locally. The decision to purchase these databases must be based on a careful consideration of their full costs balanced against the service benefits. Costs should include the increased system capacity required to store, process, and retrieve the data. The costs could include the actual sale price of the data from the publisher, and the costs of the retrieval software, processing this data to conform to local system requirements, storage in the local system, maintenance, and future updates. These should be weighed against the improvements in patron access to the information, the savings possible from no longer purchasing the information in paper or CD-ROM format, and the staff time and online charges saved by no longer using the online source. Generally speaking, it is rarely cheaper to mount a major bibliographic database in a local system, unless the information had been purchased in multiple copies and formats before switching to the locally mounted format. Some small bibliographic and full text databases, and locally produced data files may be very cost-effective to distribute in a library system. Careful analysis of all the costs involved in mounting an online file provides the information necessary to judge the cost-effectiveness of this approach to that of purchasing electronic information in this format. Despite the possibility of increased costs for locally mounted databases, the improved access and patron service may well be worth it.

E. Software

Software is a group of instructions that directs computers to function in specific ways. Computers can not operate without some form of software. There is an immense variety of software available in the marketplace, however a significant portion of this market falls outside of the collecting interests of most libraries. Programs that provide specific applications, such as those used to manage medical and dental offices, banks, retail sales, etc., are rarely collected by most libraries. Software can be classified in four basic types:

1. Operating systems

The first type of software encompasses operating systems such as DOS that provide the operating environment for computers. These programs provide the basic instructions as to how a computer can store, format, and retrieve information. Although this type of software can do basic operations such as formatting disks, creating directories, copying files, and other similar functions, most users will

6

require other "application" programs in order to make full use of computers. Many of the functions of application programs can be performed by operating systems, but this requires a great deal of programming skill on the part of a user.

2. Programming tools and languages

The second type of software is programming tools and languages. BASIC, Fortran, and C are some well known representatives of this group. These programs allow users to create their own specific computer applications. Simply stated, programming tools are languages that a computer can speak. They differentiate from application programs such as Lotus or WordPerfect in that those applications represent a prepackaged set of instructions in some language, whereas the programming tools are a free form of a computer language. Use of this group of software requires a basic understanding of computer programming and a specific knowledge of the particular tool being used. This group of software is generally used to perform specific functions that are not available in prepackaged software.

3. Application programs

The third type of software is the application programs, and these comprise the largest portion of the commercial software market. Within this group are a wide variety of programs: personal applications such as spreadsheets, word processors, database management systems, and desktop publishers; research tools for sophisticated statistical analysis and modeling; educational programs that provide computer-assisted instruction; business-oriented software that provides accounting and data management services and computer-aided design and manufacturing (CAD/CAM); and entertainment software that includes arcade-type video games. Application programs are generally of greatest interest to library users as these enable a computer to perform sophisticated operations without much training for the user.

4. Data files

The fourth type of software is data files. These are informational in nature. Programs generally perform a function utilizing some type of information. Data files represent raw information. In most situations some form of retrieval system, or at minimum an operating system, will be required to use data files. These files may include numeric data, bibliographic information, or the full text of a work such as a book, encyclopedia, or dictionary.

7

5. Shareware

Shareware is a type of software that would be a subgroup of all four basic classifications. It is most often in the public domain and has few restrictions regarding use. Unless it is copyrighted, it can be copied at will and distributed without the normal limitations of commercial products. The publisher of copyrighted shareware relies upon free copying to market the product. Often, the user is asked to register use of the product and pay a small fee. Sometimes this payment entitles the user to the benefits of future upgrades, improved documentation, and support for the use of the product.

Software is available from many sources. It can be purchased directly from the publisher or through vendors. For many commercial products there will be a wide variance in the price depending upon the source of the purchase and who is purchasing the software. Small local retail computer stores generally will be more expensive than national chains, and mail- order vendors are cheaper than both. Some software is available to libraries at special educational discounts and these can greatly reduce the cost of software. If multiple copies are going to be purchased, it may be cost-effective to purchase a site license, which generally allows a certain number of copies of the software to be distributed within the organization at a cost much lower than the cost of individual copies. When searching for a source for software, all of these options should be explored before ordering.

An integral part of the decision process involved with the purchase of software concerns the environment intended for the use of the product. Environmental concerns such as whether the software is going to be used in a mainframe, personal computer, or a network, and the basic hardware requirements should be considered before the source for purchase is selected and the item is ordered. The license agreement and the cost of software may vary if the product is intended to be run in a network. If the software is intended to be circulated, make sure the license agreement governing the use of the item does not place restrictions on this use. (It is recommended that master copies not be circulated, for instance, so a restriction on copying the software may rule out circulating the material.) It may be necessary to contact the publisher and renegotiate the standard license agreement to ensure that the intended use is in full compliance with the publisher's reservations on usage. For an in-depth discussion of the issues involved in the selection and circulation of software see Brady, Rockman, and Walch's "Software for Patron Use in Libraries: Physical Access" (see Sources for Further Information).

III.   Selection

With the advent of electronic formats, the selection process has become more complex. Added to the traditional criteria associated with collection development policy and user needs are new concerns related to technology, costs for the same information in different formats, additional staffing needs, and additional user demands. Some of the issues and questions a library should address are outlined below.

A.   Selection Criteria

1. Policy concerns

a. The criteria for selecting material in electronic format should reflect the library's own collection development and acquisitions policies.

b. It is very important to have written procedures for selecting electronic resources. It could become necessary to have different procedures for every type of format available.

c. Licensing constraints and limitations on the use of the data imposed by vendors, publishers, or producers should be addressed in the process of selection.

d. User and programmatic needs are a prime consideration. Special attention could be given to products that provide coverage of underrepresented or high-priority subject areas.

e. Selection procedures and criteria should be evaluated and revised regularly.

f. Public demand for and use of current printed versions are sometimes good indicators of the need for the electronic product.

g. The reputation of the publisher and producer should be investigated. Request a list of current customers from the publisher and contact those that seem to have the most in common with your library. Sometimes networks, consortia, and state libraries serve as clearing houses for information on new products.

h. Assess the comprehensiveness and scope of the data's coverage, and data and indexing accuracy. Reviews are helpful in this area.

i. Another important concern is the timeliness of updates or cumulations.

j. Evaluate the relative difficulty of using the printed version versus the electronic counterpart.

k. There are no standards addressing the preservation of electronic media yet. The selector must evaluate the durability of the medium and what the cost/benefit trade-off will be between immediate usefulness and potential degradation of electronic data.

2. Service concerns

   a. The selection criteria should conform with the institution's general plans for establishing a computerized information environment.
   b. Public service staffing and training levels should be evaluated in light of the additional information services available to patrons.
   c. User-friendly features such as online tutorials should be available.
   d. The user documentation should be accurate, easy to use, comprehensive, and cost-effective.
   e. The impact on current library staffing and training, such as cataloging and processing subscriptions in different formats, should be carefully assessed.
   f. Effectiveness of data retrieval software (the search engine) should be appraised.
   g. Product evaluation, such as reviews, user studies, and product demos should be consulted.
   h. The availability of printing facilities (remote or connected directly to each work station) should be considered.

3. Technical concerns

   a. A crucial concern relates to the necessity for technical support and maintenance of the product.
   b. The evaluation of software should focus on issues that include menu-driven vs. command-driven feature, override capability in the program's command structure, short initial learning curve, security (tampering and viruses), compatibility with existing hardware and software medium.
   c. The hardware related concerns include reliability, maintenance, compatibility with peripherals, flexibility for other uses or networking, security from theft and tampering.
   d. Compatibility with existing systems in the library and with the systems used by the parent organization's community should be a consideration.
   e. The environmental and spatial requirements for equipment and workstations need special consideration.

4. Cost considerations

   a. Short-term preservation benefits of optical disk technology are apparent.

   b. If print sources or other formats are discontinued there may be savings. Duplication of information in several formats usually results in higher costs (see e., below). Package discounts are sometimes available when retaining the subscription to the paper or alternate (i.e., microfiche) format.

   c. There are cost differentials between online and CD-ROM options.

   d. Information may be available in more cost-effective electronic formats.

   e. Purchase or lease options need to be studied.

   f. Plan for any additional costs for future updates or upgrades.

   g. There may be additional start-up and maintenance costs that are not reflected in the invoice for the information product. These could include site preparation and hardware shipping and installation.

   h. Consider the shelf life of the product's storage medium and replacement costs.

   i. Explore the availability of vendor/publisher discounts for hardware and software packages (bundles) associated with the product.

B. Areas of Particular Emphasis for Selection Concerns

Although hardware and software selection concerns are separated in this section, it should be recognized that both are usually covered by a single selection decision. Sometimes there is no choice, as when the publisher requires a certain software and hardware package or configuration. Many CD-ROM products are packaged this way.

The key is to examine local needs first, then find the best options.

1. Defining local needs

   Issues to be considered include:

   a. Which subject areas have a demonstrated need for specific information products in electronic format.

   b. Patron and staff groups that will benefit the most from the use of these products.

   c. The ease of use and depth of information levels appropriate for the intended user group.

   d. The comparison of the product under consideration with the scope and cost of other resources, electronic or not, currently available.

   e. Location issues such as whether the new electronic sources go to reference or similar non-circulating collections or to the stacks.

Hardware and security concerns influence these decisions.

   f. A policy that clearly specifies the conditions and procedures used to circulate this material.

   g. The practical consequences of making the selection such as cancellation of other titles or special equipment needs that may require funding.

2. Software selection considerations

Software can perform two general functions. It can act as the bridge between hardware and the information product, or it can be the information product itself, which allows users to manipulate their own data. An example of the former is the SilverPlatter search software, which provides a common command structure for searching databases from different sources. Examples of the latter are DOS, Lotus 1-2-3, or Pro-Cite.

One of the most critical issues to be considered relates to the search software the product needs in order to operate. Factors include: (1) ease of use, friendliness, online help screens, is it menu- or command-driven, are there different levels of commands available (i.e., beginners, advanced, etc.), is there a user-support service (800 number, extended hours of availability) set up by the publisher; and (2) capabilities available, such as Boolean searching, keyword/relational searching, subject searching, truncation, speed of searching, introductory documentation, etc.

The selection of all types of software should be based on criteria similar to those that govern selection for print collections and should fall within the general guidelines for the development of the collections. The users' needs should be the paramount concern when selecting software. Money spent on unused software is wasted as the shelf life of most software is very short. The purchase decision should not be based on a possibility of future use.

In addition to the general criteria used to select materials, there are other special considerations that must be addressed as part of the selection process. When purchasing software for specific needs, it is generally recommended that the buyer first select the software, then choose hardware that can run the software. This principle breaks down in the library environment because of the wide variety of software to choose from and the variety of hardware that users operate. The general hardware environment of an organization and its clients or patrons will help determine the types of software that will be selected. Elementary and secondary schools may operate in a hardware environment dominated by the use of Apple computers. Although some IBM/DOS-based software may be superior to the Apple counterpart, selection of DOS software would be inappropriate in the Apple environment. Users may not have easy access to hardware or the experience necessary to operate the software.

Beyond considerations of the hardware environment, of primary importance is the ability of the software to do what it is intended to do. Do not assume that a software product can do something if the publisher's documentation or product reviews do not describe that capability. If in doubt, contact the publisher. Next should be the consideration of how well the software can perform. These considerations should include response time, ease of use, documentation, output (both printed and downloaded information) limits on the amount of information the software can handle, and the ability to accept information from other sources. These items apply generally to software programs. Data files have a different set of considerations that include the format, structure, and organization of the data; the ability to search and retrieve the data; the ease of use; and the quality of the documentation.

The cost of software is a necessary part of selection criteria, but software pricing is more complicated than the pricing of printed materials. Before purchase it should be determined if there are other less expensive programs that meet your needs. Some software performs at relatively the same level, but has wide price variations. As usual, at the retail level there are different prices available for the same item from different sources. To complicate this issue further, there is a price structure for some products that varies depending upon whether the buyer is an educational institution, whether the buyer will use the product in a network, and whether the buyer purchases a site license for multiple copies of the product. All of these considerations should be addressed before arriving at the real cost of the product.

3. Hardware selection considerations

When purchasing new hardware, the actual acquisition may be performed outside of a library's acquisition department as this may be a capital expenditure and will be handled through a purchasing office. Hardware represents an important aspect of selection criteria. As mentioned before, the physical environment should be considered when selecting software. Some software is designed to run on specific systems. If these systems are not currently supported, there may be significant costs involved with the purchase and maintenance of the new hardware both in financial terms and in terms of staff time required to learn to operate the system. When selecting new hardware there are concerns that should be addressed. The system requirements for the software that will run on the hardware should be matched to the configuration of the computer. These normally involve the amount of memory, disk storage, video display capabilities, and type of processor available.

Once the requirements are established one should determine what is available in the marketplace. Some software applications will run on only certain machines and this narrows the list to a few choices, while commercially available software that runs in the DOS environment will run on a variety of IBM products and "clones" of the IBM personal computer. There is a wide price range for these machines. Warranties, company reputation, and on-site service should be considered when evaluating the cost of any machine. Another consideration when selecting hardware should be the use of local area networks. If several machines are being considered or more efficient use is required of existing hardware, the use of a local area network could provide some savings especially if peripherals such as printers and high density storage can be shared. The use of a local area network could require rethinking the software selected as some software is difficult or impossible to use in a networked environment, or additional charges may be added to purchase a network license.

Before a final decision to purchase is made, the hardware requirements need to be evaluated. Internal purchasing policies may affect how the purchase of hardware is handled. This may be a capital expenditure budgeted separately and purchased by a unit outside the acquisitions department. Information products that come bundled with hardware could be problematic in respect to units that divide purchases along strict lines. Some major points to consider:

a. Current and anticipated demand for the information and the overall costs. The quality of service is directly related to the amount of money available to support hardware capable of providing fast-running workstations for many users.
b. Ascertaining that the desired information can be run on currently available computers is important. Issues include:

   (1) Overall system compatibility. Some products designed for one type of computer won't run on other equipment.

14

(2) Hardware configuration—memory, disk storage, processor speed, etc.

(3) Need for software platforms to interface with the data.

(4) Compatibility of current CD-ROM drives.

c. Growth in the size of the product may affect the hardware configuration in the near future. As the database grows it may be necessary to add more disk storage, memory, CD-ROM drives, etc., to maintain the resource.

d. Cost-effectiveness of the purchase option may be affected by whether it comes bundled with the hardware or not.

e. Hardware costs should include the cost of maintenance contracts.

f. The purchase of new hardware may require the following:

(1) Space for the new equipment and additional electrical and telecommunications wiring.

(2) Costs for start-up/site preparation.

(3) More staff time for technical and training support.

(4) Costs for supplies such as printers, paper, ribbons, etc.

g. Whether the library will supply the necessary hardware to use videotapes, disks, games, etc.

h. The integrity of circulation copies of electronic information will need to be assessed when the material is returned. Hardware should be available for staff use in screening returned materials for damage or software viruses.

4. Storage (short- and long-term)

The local storage of electronic media is greatly affected by the license agreements governing the use of each product as well as local resources that can be used to pay for the storage of and access to the products. Approaches to storage are as vast as the variety of products available. Considerations include:

a. Archival copies of all types of software should be made and kept off-site for long-term storage. Computer centers are best equipped to handle this type of storage.

b. Software that is used in-house should be loaded onto a hard disk drive and back-ups kept separately for the short term.

c. Circulating software should be kept in proper protective containers that prevent damage to the disks as they are transported by patrons.

d. Software and all other media such as videotapes and games should be stored as far as possible from sources of electromagnetic radiation such as telephones, some theft-detection systems, and even some systems terminals.

e. Long-term storage for some products such as CD-ROMs is usually not a problem as the information is leased and not owned.

f. Use CD-ROM drives that require the use of specially designed disc carriers (caddies) and keep the CD-ROM discs in these caddies.

g. The ideal approach to short-term storage of CD-ROMs is to place the discs in a "jukebox" and access the information through an individual workstation or a network of workstations.

   (1) CD-ROMs are not indestructible and constant handling and usage will cut down on disc longevity.

   (2) This storage method is expensive as the hardware used is costly, and if LANs are used staff will be needed to maintain the network. There are normally extra license fees for CD-ROMs mounted in networks.

5. Shareware

Shareware presents fewer problems to libraries as these materials are not under copyright protection. There are no restrictions on the copying or circulation of such software. The developers of these software programs generally utilize the sharing of the programs to market the product. If users decide to use the programs they are encouraged to register and pay a small fee to the producers. There is no way for the producers to ensure that users of the software comply with a request for registration, but generally users are encouraged by additional benefits ensured by registration. Shareware is available in regular computer disk format and as CD-ROMs. If used in a circulating collection, shareware programs should be copied from masters and as the disks are returned, they should be re-formatted and a new copy placed on the disk from the master. This will prevent computer viruses from being transmitted by these disks. It will also prevent changes made by a borrower from interfering with the future use of the program.

6. Local area networks (LANs)

A local area network is a linked combination of software, computers, and peripherals such as printers, high capacity storage devices, and CD-ROM drives that share information and the use of the peripherals. Local area networks are a popular means to increase the efficiency of a series of computers, especially small personal computers. In a single workstation setting, many peripherals such as printers and high capacity storage devices are not in constant use. These peripherals have a greater capacity for use than is normally available in a single machine. By linking several machines, the use of these peripherals can be shared, greatly reducing the cost of the network when compared to the cost of an equal number of individual workstations similarly equipped. There are many possible uses of LANs to access information in electronic format. Some software can be mounted in the system and several users can work with the program at the same time. Multiple CD-ROM drives can be attached, and several users can use the same product at the same time or access a series of different CD-ROMs from the same workstation. The use of LAN technology can greatly expand patron access to electronic information used in the system.

Before jumping into the creation of LANs for the purpose of supporting multiple users of electronic products, several points must be considered:

    a.   Not all software and CD-ROMs can be networked. Select products that are desired by your organization—then ascertain if these can be used in a LAN.

    b.   Determine if there are added costs for networking the products and weigh these costs against the cost of individual workstation applications.

    c.   Hardware and the LAN system software must be considered. After selecting what products are to be run in the system, choose hardware and LAN software that can best support these uses.

    d.   LANs require staff to be available to set up the system and maintain it. LANs are notorious for being easy to render temporarily inoperable in public use settings.

Local area networks can greatly improve the efficiency of a series of computers and peripherals and can improve access to some products. These improvements must be weighed against the increased cost of network licenses for some products and the necessity of having trained staff available to maintain the system. An excellent source for information on local area networks is William Saffady's *Local Area Networks: A Survey of the Technology* (see Sources for Further Information).

7. Access or ownership

The dilemma of "access or ownership" has been precipitated by the huge increase in information available in electronic format and a profusion of systems used to market the information. Products in electronic format offer access to a wide variety of resources not always owned by the library. These electronic products themselves may be leased or shared in a consortium, not "owned" by a library.

Traditionally, interlibrary loan services satisfied patrons' demands for material not available in the local library. Now, information not available locally can be obtained in a number of ways. Some electronic information sources provide either a full or a truncated version of text or a database on a local system or the information can be accessed online. One of the major decision points to be considered when purchasing electronic information products involves the question of whether the item should be purchased and stored locally, networked in a wide area or regional network, or accessed online on an "as needed" basis. As technology and the marketing of information products advance, decisions made today may be obsolete tomorrow.

Some vendors are aggressively marketing online access to remote databases through the use of networked "user-friendly" gateways. Also, the development of standards for sharing electronic information such as Z39.50, a NISO communication protocol, will ease gateway use. These developments could make investment in large indexes based on CD-ROM or mounted in local computer system a difficult financial decision, especially when the total cost of local hardware, storage, and maintenance is considered. On the other hand the purchase of the hardware and software could be used to support other future ventures in electronic publishing as more full text and interactive text/video/audio publications are produced on CD-ROM and as sophisticated full text data systems become available for local use.

The current and anticipated needs of a library's users balanced against the library's resources should dictate the decision to purchase or to provide access to information resources. Some issues that should be considered when deciding the ownership/access formula for any particular library include:

a. The percentage of the materials budget that should be allocated to the acquisition of traditional print and non-print materials, locally owned electronic information products, and electronic access to outside sources.

18

b. The sources of revenue for the development of full text or document delivery services.
c. Staff training for the efficient use of new electronic sources.
d. Availability of backfiles for a one-time cost rather than included as part of a continuing annual fee. Usually the one-time purchase is cheaper, but the purchase of backfiles must be carefully considered against the local costs of storing the information.
e. Important legal aspects that govern the local use of electronic products, such as copyright restrictions on downloading information from databases and limiting access to the product through passwords.

8. User participation and assessment of user needs

Library staff and library patrons can play an important part in the selection process for electronic resources. Media in electronic format has a much shorter shelf life than standard printed materials. Most scholarly books and serials are printed on quality paper and a library can expect these items to be useful one hundred to two hundred years from now. If recent history is a guide, some types of electronic resources may become obsolete in ten or fifteen years. The technology and software that operate the resource may become outdated and unuseable. Expenditures in this area must have a high rate of patron acceptance in the short term to be considered cost-effective.

There are a number of ways to involve users in the selection process. If preview copies of an item are available, acquire these and give staff and patrons a chance to use the product before purchasing. Before accepting a review copy, read carefully all agreements that govern the use and return of the item as a library may be liable for the full cost of the item if not returned within a specified time. Encourage staff and patrons to visit preview centers to review copies of a product before purchase, allowing them an opportunity to work with an item, providing a clear feedback channel to selectors. Another way staff and users can obtain information that would aid them in evaluating a product is by checking electronic bulletin boards and contacting user groups. By communicating with these types of groups, staff and users can discuss a product with other individuals that have used it before and do not necessarily have an interest in "selling" the item. A further option, to preview a potential acquisition, is to volunteer the library as a beta test site, the second, or field test step in the development process. By previewing products, librarians can also have some impact on their final design. Sometimes vendors and publishers also offer significant discounts to beta test sites.

9. Preservation

The preservation of information purchased in electronic format is a function of a rapidly evolving technology. Printed materials have a reasonably certain shelf life if not subjected to careless usage. This is not so for electronic media. In ten or twenty years the hardware used to access this media may undergo radical changes. Unless a publisher constantly upgrades a product to keep pace with technological advances, libraries may find themselves archiving hardware as well as information products to ensure future use.

There is no guarantee that materials produced using current technology will be accessible indefinitely into the future. No one expects to be using the same computers and CD-ROM drives ten to twenty years from now.

Collections of videotapes and games may become obsolete as users move to newer technology and the current items can no longer be used. Since these materials generally cannot be legally copied and reformatted these collections may be considered as disposable. Preservation concerns will be especially important for full text materials and certain video products that are published on a one-time basis. If hardware to access the product is not maintained, other solutions will have to be sought. It may be possible to re-format some information for newer technology. But the publisher may restrict that feasibility if it sees an opportunity to re-format the product and sell it again.

The issue of preserving information in electronic format transcends the concerns of libraries as much broader issues exist. What will happen to data stored by governmental and corporate bodies in electronic format? Will this information be inaccessible to everyone in the future? Long-term preservation of electronic data is not yet a reality and the players that drive developments in this area probably won't be libraries. Awareness of this will allow libraries to set policies now that may mitigate the impact of preservation issues in the future. Before migrating from one generation of hardware to another, carefully assess the impact this will have on the information products currently in use. This consideration will be especially important as information migrates from local area networks to other networks and as new advanced integrated library systems are implemented.

10. Standards

Libraries should carefully assess a publisher's compliance with national standards and the intended local use of particular products before purchasing an item. Not all aspects of electronic publishing are covered by ANSI or ISO standards. As this industry is quickly evolving, some products will be available long before standards governing them are established. Users should determine which standards are applicable to their use of the product, then determine if those standards are met by a publisher.

11. Initial release concerns

Frequently, new products contain bugs that have not been detected by the producer. Software is particularly prone to this syndrome. Caution is advised before acquiring a new product as most electronic information products are expensive. In some situations a library may find itself buying a second release of an item to correct shortcomings in the first purchase. Product reviews are common in the appropriate literature and these will identify the bugs and shortcomings of a new offering. To delay purchase of an item until it has been assessed by professional reviewers is a prudent course of action when acquiring electronic formats.

IV. Acquisitions

The acquisition of materials in electronic format does present some different considerations. Standard acquisition practices are not covered in great detail; rather the intent is to focus on aspects of the acquisition process that require a fresh approach.

A. Major Acquisitions Issues

1. Lease and purchase agreements

Often, information in electronic format is leased instead of sold. For a fee, the publisher allows the subscriber to use the product during a specified period of time in specific ways. Some publishers will offer both lease and license agreements and it will be necessary to determine which arrangement best suits an organization's needs. Frequently, as new information is published and received, the older data needs to be returned to the publisher or destroyed. When the purchase agreement ends, all data returns to the publisher. Before ordering be sure that all terms of the purchase or lease arrangements are clear. All changes in terms should be negotiated with the publisher before purchasing. Often, publishers are willing to modify lease agreements if changes are necessary before libraries can purchase an item. Negotiating with a publisher of electronic information is never unproductive even if it does not result in changes in a lease agreement. The publisher will become more aware of the needs of libraries and may be more attuned to the library market in the future. If compliance with an agreement is difficult or impossible, refrain from purchasing or leasing the item. If an item is purchased through a vendor or supplier, remember that the vendor is a second party and its interpretation of a lease may not be binding. Often publishers do not offer uniform agreements for all their products. Careful reading of lease agreements is strongly recommended. Items to consider should include:

    a. The lease should clearly delineate the terms of the ownership or lease agreements. This should include a description (if applicable) of what backfiles are being acquired, the ownership of these backfiles, how often updates are to be received, and the disposition of superseded files.

    b. Be sure all licensing, usage, or copyright restrictions are indicated. The intended use of a product within an organization may be severely restricted by rights reserved to the publisher.

    c. If hardware is included in the purchase, the agreement should state whether the machinery is leased or purchased. If hardware is included in the lease, the maintenance responsibility should be addressed. If the seller provides maintenance, the terms of the service should be defined (i.e., the computer will be repaired or replaced in twenty-four hours).

    d. Product warranties need to be clearly stated and understood.

2. Documentation

The manuals or thesauri supplied with a product are important aspects of an electronic publication. Electronic texts that are simply manuscripts in a digitized format may require very simple explanations before use. Large data sets that use special software to organize and retrieve the information could require the use of extensive manuals and thesauri before using. The quality of information provided to instruct the user in the operation of a product can enhance the value of a system or greatly detract from its usefulness. Documentation need not be in a printed format. Many systems offer quality instructions and online help as an integral part of their package. A good source for information detailing the documentation of a product would be found in product reviews or the publisher's documentation. Often there are software guides and manuals available separately from the one that comes with the product. These are independently prepared and usually written after the release of the product. They are widely available in software stores.

Usefulness of publishers' documentation has a direct relation to the computer literacy level of staff and users. A very knowledgeable staff and clientele will require fewer training guides, and the need for high-level documentation becomes less of a concern. However, poor documentation will greatly reduce the overall acceptance and effectiveness of information in electronic format. The friendliness of the documentation may influence the actual location of the electronic source in relation to the proximity of personal assistance in the library.

The Machine-Assisted Reference Section (MARS) Products and Services Committee of ALA's Reference and Adult Services Division has prepared a "Checklist of Items for Inclusion in CD-ROM Vendor Documentation," which appeared in the Winter 1993 issue of *RQ* (vol. 33, no. 2: 215–17).

3. Warranties

There is a wide range in warranties provided for electronic formats and the hardware that supports them. Some products are fully warranted against theft or damage, others carry no warranty at all and must be replaced at full cost if problems arise. Most software publishers allow for the creation of full backups of their product; consequently, no warranty is needed. However, in some cases, publishers place restrictions on the number. The purchasers may find themselves in need of a replacement if they require more than the allowed number of backups. Some hardware comes with full maintenance included in the cost of the system, others with no maintenance or warranty at all.

For other types of media such as CD-ROM and videotapes, policies will vary from the full replacement of a title if the item is lost, stolen, or damaged, to a very restrictive approach in which the user would need to repurchase the product under the same circumstances. Current technology makes the full-scale copying of many CD-ROMs and videodiscs nearly impossible. Even if this were possible, the copyright and license restrictions would probably forbid the full scale copying of a CD-ROM product. The user is completely dependent on the publisher for replacement of the item if it is lost, stolen, or damaged in the future.

4. Licensing (including site licenses)

Most publishers of information in electronic format will restrict the use of their products through the use of license agreements. These agreements must be carefully reviewed by library staff before the product is purchased. Frequently, especially with software, the license agreement is written on the product and by breaking the seal, the user agrees to accept the license as stated. This is often referred to as a "shrinkwrap" license. The provisions of licenses will vary from very restrictive to very liberal. Many agreements go well beyond the scope of the protection provided by the Copyright Revision Act. By accepting the license agreement the user is contractually bound to these restrictions. However, in some circumstances, there are overriding rights to any software agreement in favor of the purchaser. These include the right to make an archival copy, the right of a library to make the software available as part of a public service (this may not be the case in corporate libraries not governed by educational fair-use doctrine), and the right to make adaptations in the program in order to run a program. These rights do not apply to all information products in electronic format. CD-ROMs, videodiscs and tapes, video games, and other products frequently can't be copied for archival purposes.

Licenses grant only those rights that are spelled out in the document; all others are assumed to be reserved to the producer. If a license agreement appears to be too restrictive, contact the publisher and negotiate more suitable terms.

Before entering into any license agreement, be sure that local protocols have been properly followed to ensure the legality of the contract. Some organizations do not empower libraries or their acquisitions departments to enter into some forms of legally binding contracts. It is best to read all licenses carefully and not to assume that a publisher licenses all products in the same manner. Items generally addressed in the license are:

   a. Restrictions on the use of the data in regard to the copying, printing, or downloading from the database.
   b. Restrictions on the number of simultaneous users, or the use of the product in local (LAN) and wide (WAN) area networks. If a system can accommodate multiple users, extra costs are frequently involved.

24

c. Restrictions on the method of access, such as dial-access or Internet.

d. Conversion of the database to other media.

e. Limits on use to internal or non-commercial activities.

f. Limits on the ability to transfer, resell, or reassign the product.

g. For software, limiting the program to use on one machine by one user at a time.

h. Restrictions that limit access to the subscriber's patrons and staff.

i. Requirements that the library guarantee the integrity of circulating copies of full text items.

5. Copyright

The field of electronic publishing is changing rapidly and the issue of how the current copyright laws affect all aspects of this industry are not absolutely clear. The fair-use doctrine applies to information in electronic format as it applies to printed materials. Fair use allows the downloading or copying of information for educational and research purposes. Guidelines for printed materials have been established to define the percentage of a work that may be copied for educational purposes. But it is not clear where the line is drawn regarding fair use of information in electronic format. For most purposes, libraries already place limits that generally fall within fair use guidelines on the use of electronic information. Because of high demand, most CD-ROM use and online searching are limited to small intervals that do not give the user the opportunity to copy or download amounts of information that could be questioned under fair use doctrine. As locally mounted databases become more prevalent this informal control may be lost and it may become necessary for libraries in educational settings to clearly display messages informing users of what constitutes fair use of the information available in the system. Educate patrons as to what is generally accepted as fair use. Messages on local systems certainly won't stop a determined user but can reduce the liability of the library and prevent the unintentional violation of copyright.

In most situations, the publisher of electronic formats will define what they consider to be fair use of their product through the use of license agreements if they are concerned that general copyright does not protect the use of their product. Some publishers place limits in their systems that make downloading of extremely large portions of the data virtually impossible. The issue of copyright for electronic formats is one that will remain unclear for most libraries until these issues are addressed through legislative action. Be sure that all license agreements with publishers are enforced. Do not make software available to more than one user at a time unless specifically allowed to do so. If an issue is unclear and in dispute, use great caution before committing to a course of action.

B. Mechanics of the Order Process

Materials in electronic formats can be published as either monographs or as serials. The actual mechanics of the order process for electronic formats differ little from the standard methods established for books and serials. As with their printed counterparts, there are distinct differences in the way serials and monographs are processed, and this *Guide* will describe only the most basic details. The ALA acquisition guidelines for monographs and serials are listed in the appended bibliography, and these should be referred to for supplementary information on the mechanics of ordering materials.

1. Standard information on the order form

Whether the purchase order is mailed, sent as a fax or via electronic computer-to-computer transmission, it should supply clearly labeled information. The information for describing products in electronic formats includes:

a. Title, authorship, or statement of responsibility
b. Edition statement
c. Publishing information or imprint
d. Any numbering system associated with the specific item being ordered, such as ISBN, ISSN, bar code/product code, vendor or publisher inventory numbers
e. The purchase order number
f. Order date
g. Number of copies requested
h. Variant ship-to and bill-to locations.

Additional considerations for continuing orders (including serials) are:

a. Volume numbering
b. Coverage of backfiles ordered
c. Frequency of new issues
d. Length of subscription and subscription dates.

In some automated systems, data codes can be established that record the specific format of the material ordered. This can be an important management tool. One drawback is that new codes will have to be added to existing ordering systems as new formats are introduced. Rush procedures may include a system-supplied note on the order form. Additionally, information important to the ordering library such as special handling-on-arrival instructions, a requestor's name, the estimated price, the fund, and the library location may be stored by the system. If special fields are not available for these items (especially requestor) this information may be recorded as internal notes if the acquisitions system has this feature.

2. Special instructions or information on the order form

The above information parallels that used for most purchases. Information in electronic format will require the inclusion of special types of information in order to expedite the fulfillment of an order:

    a. Specify the exact type of computer (IBM, Apple, etc.) and disk drive (5.25- or 3.5-inch; double or high density) that the product will run on.

    b. Bundled hardware or software should be clearly described on the order.

        (1) RAM capacity
        (2) Hard and floppy drives, and size of disks that can be accommodated
        (3) Monitor
        (4) Software to be included (DOS, Windows, etc.)
        (5) Keyboard style, mouse, etc.

    c. If a publisher's license agreement places vague restrictions on the use of the item, include a message to the vendor stipulating the library's intent to circulate the material, or load it on a network, or make the item available to remote sites.

It may be useful to place separate orders for the same product to differentiate between a backfile and a continuing order. The backfile would represent a one-time purchase. The order for the updates would be a serial type order and would continue into the foreseeable future. The anticipated future cost of the product would be based upon payments made on the serial record. The expenditure for the backfile should not be used in cost projections.

Electronically formatted products should be ordered according to the normal flow to maintain processing efficiency at both ends of the transactions. Vendors or publishers of electronic formats often deal only in those formats and their volume is much less than a major book or serial publisher. Consequently, a library can expect a faster rate of order fulfillment, with turnaround occurring anywhere between four to eight weeks. If items are needed in less time, the library should expedite the process by communicating directly with the publisher. Some publishers will accept orders over the telephone, requesting a purchase order number, and shipping with a "pro forma" invoice. Be careful to include all necessary items of information when placing phone orders and to record these orders on your system. Rush procedures can also be worked out in advance with vendors.

3. Receipt and payment arrangements

The library may want to separate funds for materials in electronic formats in order to track expenditures in these emerging areas for budget planning and allocation review purposes. In many situations, the start-up cost for a product may be more significant than the costs needed to pay for periodic updates. The purchase of substantial backfiles greatly increases the initial costs, consequently the first year's charges cannot be used to indicate future costs and expenditure reports may not be a good predictor for the next year's budget.

The procedures associated with the receipt and payment for items in electronic format are very similar to that for books and serials.

   a. All items received need to be carefully compared against the order to ensure that the item received is what was ordered.
   b. Individuals receiving materials should not break the shrink-wrap until someone has had a chance to review the packaging for a license.
   c. Dependent upon the return privileges granted by each vendor, the library may want to delay payment until the material is reviewed for defects. Damage to printed materials is fairly obvious but damage or defects in electronic information will need closer inspection and use to detect.

Publishers or producers may require prepayment before shipment. This practice sometimes causes problems for libraries, either from slow fulfillment tying up funds for extended periods, or from outright fraud when the item that was ordered is never shipped. Libraries are encouraged to stay informed about potential problems with certain companies, and to never ship substantial prepayments to unfamiliar P.O. boxes or organizations.

4. Claims

As currency of coverage is quite important with some electronic products it may be necessary to establish a separate claim cycle for these items. If an order remains unfilled after a long period of time, it may be prudent to check with the publisher for the availability of newer versions of the product. The claim period can be programmed into many automated acquisitions systems, so that claims are generated on a regular basis for unfilled orders.

5. Cancellations

Libraries should set up regular procedures and routines when canceling orders with vendors or publishers. These may include:

   a. Agreeing on a time period beyond which the order will be considered canceled.
   b. The library may choose to cancel outstanding orders after the initial claim period expires.
   c. Some cancellations involve titles that are received on a continuing basis and the process will be similar to canceling serials.
   d. Some leased or licensed electronic products will require the return of all materials, including disks, tapes, etc., to the publisher.

6. Returns

Items will have to be returned from time to time for a number of reasons, including:

   a. Duplicate receipt of materials
   b. Incorrect materials sent by the publisher
   c. Defective copies
   d. Publisher's requirements (e.g., superseded CD-ROMs)

Communicate precisely the nature of the problem and why the item is being returned. While the vast majority of publishers and vendors are reasonable in their approaches to these problems, there are some problematic companies. Be selective when choosing a source for purchase, as cheap mail-order houses or cut-rate hardware producers may appear inexpensive on the surface but turn out to be expensive in the end.

7. Review copies

Information in electronic format is often some of the most expensive titles that libraries buy. It is common practice in some sectors of the industry to ship items on approval or as review copies. Sometimes the review copy is a sample of the product and presents the basic system and a few test records. This type of review copy rarely causes any problems as they are either very cheap to purchase, or are sent gratis and are disposable. This is not the case in other situations, and the review copy is the actual product and is usually accompanied by a notice that the item must be returned by a specified date or it will be considered purchased by the library. The notice becomes an invoice in many cases after the review period expires. Avoid accepting material on this basis if there is potential difficulty in the length of the review period. You may want to negotiate a longer period before or immediately after receipt.

8. Leasing and rental agreements

Many producers want to keep control over the data used as the basis for their electronic media. To protect their ownership of the product the publisher will require that the user sign a lease agreement that limits the use of the product and reserves certain rights to the producer. This is especially true of software and CD-ROM indexes, where the physical media is sometimes leased to the library on a subscription basis, and the actual disc, tape, etc., remains the property of the producer or vendor. Now it is possible in some instances to negotiate retention of the material after the lease period expires. The lease agreements may stipulate who may use the product, prohibit the downloading or printing of information, and may even limit the number of users that can access the data file. Generally it is prudent to keep the actual lease agreements in a secure file. Make sure that all appropriate staff (i.e., the budget officer) have copies of this agreement. If using an automated system, put the salient points of the agreement in the acquisitions record as internal notes for quick reference. If necessary, establish a check-in record for periodic updates. In some situations it will be necessary to clarify the terms of a lease before purchasing. If this occurs during a phone conversation, be sure to include major changes as notes printed on the purchase order.

9. Discounts

The price structures used to market electronic information are complex and are much more challenging to unravel than the pricing systems used for printed materials. Discounts are irregular due to a wide variety of publishers and vendors. Publishers and vendors sometimes offer discounted prices on orders for multiple copies or for several expensive items. The acquisition of materials in electronic format is most frequently done directly with a publisher who is usually the sole source for the item. Publishers sometimes offer discounts based on volume or other considerations such as concurrent ownership of the paper or other format of a title. Negotiating directly over the telephone or in person is the best way to receive these discounts. Prepublishing discounts can substantially reduce the cost of the product. If ordering through a vendor, it is worth asking the vendor to pass on any early payment or prepayment discounts. Prepayment discounts may be available only through direct orders to the producer or publisher. Some vendors negotiate their own prepublishing or other discounts, and shopping around for vendors who do this is sometimes worth the effort. A library can also negotiate a general discount rate with a vendor if the vendor feels that the volume of business reduces costs sufficiently. Some publishers offer further discounts for items purchased by a consortia of users. The electronic publishing industry is rapidly changing and the pricing structures for product lines shifts accordingly. When negotiating prices don't assume that a quote made several weeks ago will be current.

Glossary

American Standard Code for Information Interchange (ASCII)   An adopted international standard that uses an eight-bit character code for all letters, numbers, and symbols

ANSI   American National Standards Institute

bridge   A hardware/software combination that enables you to connect one LAN to another and communicate across the connection as if it were a single entity. Some bridges enable you to connect LANs that use dissimilar communications protocols—for example, an Ethernet LAN and a token ring LAN.

CARL   Colorado Alliance of Research Libraries

CD-I (Interactive Compact Disc)   A new CD format that will allow for audio, video, and data storage on a single CD, in addition to graphics and data

CD-PROM (Compact Disc, Programmable Read Only Memory) Still in the R&D stage; intended to allow users to copy information from a CD-ROM disc

CD-ROM (Compact Disc-Read Only Memory)   A standardized CD format that stores about 550 megabytes of data on a 4.75-inch disc. Discs are "read" only and information cannot be erased or changed once the disc is made or "stamped," much like a stereo record CD audio recording.

CD-ROM LAN   A network composed of multiple microcomputer workstations, a large and powerful "file server" computer, a CD-ROM server (or linked servers), printers, the LAN and CD-ROM networking software to make it all work together, and wiring between the different components

chapter encoding   An electronic "bookmark" used on some discs to divide them into sections, allowing access within seconds to key scenes or other highlights

compact audio disc   Its primary application is sound recording. Encodes data directly in digital form rather than video's analog format.

constant angular velocity (CAV)   Standard-play format that holds a maximum of 30 minutes per side. Allows perfect still-frames, interference-free scanning (forward and reverse), and frame indexing. Discs with single-frame access to still photos in supplementary material require this format.

constant linear velocity (CLV)   Extended-play format that holds a maximum of 60 minutes per side. Only high-end laser disc players with digital memory can simulate clear scanning and freeze-frames with these discs. Other players provide visual scanning but with interference, and no still-frame capability.

CX noise reduction   Used to remove background noise from analog soundtracks (All laser discs have analog tracks; most of the newer ones also have digital tracks.)

DATA-ROM   An erasable product that would allow for permanent storage on one side of the disc—similar to CD-ROM—and erasable or write-once storage on the other

dial-up   The use of a personal computer, outside a self-contained computer system, to access that system using a modem (telephone line) or Ethernet/BITNET access

digitally mastered   A laser disc with digital sound, just like a compact disc

download   The copying or storage of electronic information from a host system to a disk or tape

electronic text   Term used to describe everything from computer-based instructional systems to word processing files, database records, electronic mail, teleconferencing, and reference books on CD-ROM

electronic texts   Computer-searchable collections that can be transmitted via disks, phone lines, or other media at a fraction of the cost in money and paper as with present-day paper media. These electronic books will not have to be reserved and restricted to use by one patron at a time. All materials will be available to all patrons from all locations at all times (Hart, Michael, "Project Gutenberg: Access to Electronic Texts," *Database*, Dec. 1990).

file server   A disk that acts as the central repository for applications and data files

gateways   An adapter inserted in a workstation on the network and connected to the host system by a direct cable or by a modem. Provides high-speed communication to a mainframe from a network. A gateway also enables the network to perform as if it were a mainframe terminal connected to the mainframe.

High Sierra Group (HSG)   Informal committee of equipment manufacturers, software developers, and information providers. The group developed a standard logical file format that specifies a directory structure and basic layout discs.

HSG file format   Format specifically designed for high performance in CD-ROM applications with many large files. It compensates for the slow access times of CD-ROM drives and facilitates product implementation under a variety of operating systems, including MS-DOS, UNIX, VMS, Apple DOS, and the Macintosh operating systems.

HyperCard   A software development system for Macintosh computers that enables the user to create programs that can link text, graphics, and media in an interactive environment

interactive video   The meshing of video and computer technologies which uses a video program (moving pictures and voice tracks) and computer programs run together so that the user's actions or choices affect the way in which the program unfolds. Used extensively in education and training.

interface   The link between two different pieces of equipment, or the link between two different systems

ISO   International Standards Organization

laserdiscs   Generic term for reflective, optical storage discs. Sizes include the 4.75-inch CD-ROM, 5.25-inch, etc. Most are not standardized.

letterboxing   A method to retain a film's original aspect ratio (width to height) when transferring it to video (disc or tape). Black areas mask out part of the television's standard 1.33:1 ratio to accommodate film ratios generally ranging from 1.66:1 to 2.35:1. Usually the film ratio is compressed at least a bit to lessen the severity of letterboxing, keeping the reduction in screen area used to a minimum.

local area network (LAN)   Workstations linked to each other; typically high-speed communication mechanisms. The term describes networked personal computers in a specific work area, that is, a department or an office. It also applies to a number of networks in various locations that are connected by a bridge, and a network that is connected to a larger computer by a direct connection or gateway.

metropolitan area network (MAN)   A network used to link LANs within a local telephone exchange.

nodes   The available connections for PCs, workstations, and peripherals that are available without further modem, multiplexer, or equipment installations other than the cable from the workstation or peripheral to the network

Online Book Initiative (OBI)   A project aimed at creating a publicly accessible repository of books, proceedings, reference works, catalogs, technical documentation, maps, and images

optical digital medium   A storage medium that most often appears in disc format, but is also being developed in tape and card formats. Most work on the optical digital disc has been directed toward the computer mass-storage market. It has only write-once and multiple-read capabilities, also called write-once, read-many, or WORM.

planning and scanning   A method for transferring wide screen films for the narrow television aspect ratio. Artificial "pans" move across the wide frame to follow (presumably) the most important action—retaining what fits within a 1.33:1 frame and cutting off the rest.

second audio track   Discs equipped with an alternate sound channel (perhaps a commentary on the picture as it's shown)

server   Any storage media node on a network, most commonly a file server

shareware   Public domain software

site license   A license agreement that normally allows unlimited usage of a product at an individual site

Small Computer Systems Interface (SCSI)   An industry standard, intelligent bus design which supports the attachment of mass storage devices, laser printers, and other high-speed peripheral equipment

Standard Generalized Markup Language (SGML)   The basis of the TEI standard (see below). Allows for the insertion of typesetting instructions, keywords, editorial comments, and other notes in angle brackets, while the body of the text remains readable as ASCII text.

terminal   A workstation connected to a mainframe or a minicomputer. PCs qualify when running terminal emulation hardware/software or as a diskless workstation.

Text Encoding Initiative (TEI)   Cooperative attempt of three associations (the Association for Computers and the Humanities, the Association for Computational Linguistics, and the Association for Literary and Linguistic Computing) to set standards. The goal is to define a format that is machine and software independent, easy to use, and compatible with existing standards.

videodisc   A videorecording on a disc, with two basic applications: as a publishing and distribution medium for general purpose "entertainment" programs such as a motion picture, and as a vehicle for interactive programs for training, education, arcade games, public information, and marketing. All the information is recorded within the audio and video format of a standard television signal.

wide area network (WAN)   Long distance networks, usually a handful of local area networks distributed geographically but connected via telecommunications links. Wide area network technology supports remote data communications needs, often extending beyond the local telephone exchange.

workstation   The personal computers on a network used to run applications and enter data, and the nodes that send the data to the file server for storage. Workstations in a local area network are complete personal computers, containing memory, processing power, and local disk drives.

WORM (write-once, read-many)   A new type of laser disc that allows for permanent storage by the users. Allows users to record original data on "blank" discs on a one-time basis only.

Sources for Further Information

CD-ROM

Carey, Joan, and Virginia Massey-Burzio. "Installing a Local Area Compact Disk Network." *C&RL News* 50, no. 11:988–91 (1989).

CD-ROM Data Bases: Catalog of Information on CD-ROM Discs. Los Angeles, Calif.: Updata Publications, 1989– .

CD-ROM Information Products: An Evaluation Guide and Directory. Ed. C. J. Armstrong and J. A. Large. Brookfield, Vt.: Gower, 1990– .

CD-ROM Librarian. Westport, Conn.: Meckler, 1987– .

CD-ROM Licensing and Copyright Issues for Libraries. (Supplement to *Computers in Libraries*, no. 11) Ed. Meta Nissley and Nancy Melin Nelson. Westport, Conn.: Meckler, 1990.

CD-ROM Local Area Networks: A User's Guide. (Supplement to *Computers in Libraries*, no. 24) Ed. Norman Desmarais. Westport, Conn.: Meckler, 1991.

CD-ROM Professional. Weston, Conn.: Pemberton Pr., 1990– .

CD-ROM Review. Peterborough, N.H.: CW Communications/Peterborough Inc., 1987– .

CD-ROM Reviews 1987–1990: Optical Product Reviews from CD-ROM Librarian. Ed. Norman Desmarais. Westport, Conn.: Meckler, 1991.

CD-ROMs in Print. Westport, Conn.: Meckler, 1987– .

Cochenour, John, and Patricia Weaver-Meyers. "CD-ROM: Practical Considerations for Libraries." *Journal of Library Administration* 9, no. 3:57–67 (1988).

Connolly, Bruce. "CD Collection Development: Sources and Tools." *Library Journal* 114:36–42 (1989).

Davis, Trisha L. "Acquisition of CD-ROM Databases for Local Area Networks." *Journal of Academic Librarianship* 19, no. 2:68–71 (1993).

Elshami, Ahmed. *CD-ROM Technology for Information Managers.* Chicago: ALA, 1990.

39

Essential Guide to CD-ROM. Westport, Conn.: Meckler, 1986.

Flanders, Bruce L. "Spinning the Hits: CD-ROM Networks in Libraries." *American Libraries* 21:32–33 (1990).

Gatten, Jeffrey, Judy Ohles, Mary Gaylord, and Harvey Soule. "Purchasing CD-ROM Products: Considerations for a New Technology." *Library Acquisitions: Practice and Theory* 11, no. 4:273–81 (1987).

Griebel, Rolf. "Problems Involved in the Purchase of Machine Readable Data Carriers with Special Reference to CD-ROM." *Bibliotheksdienst* 23:795–806 (1989).

Haar, John, Julegh Clark, Sally Jacobs, and Frank Campbell. "Choosing CD-ROM Products." *C&RL News* 51:839–841 (1990).

Hardin, Steve. "Multiple Database Access: More Users, More Considerations." *CD-ROM Professional* 4, no. 2:32–34 (1991).

Herther, Nancy K. "CD-ROM and Information Dissemination: An Update." *Online* 11, no. 2:56–64 (1987).

Jensen, Mary Brandt. "CD-ROM Licenses: What's in the Fine or Nonexistent Print May Surprise You." *CD-ROM Professional* 4, no. 2:13–16 (1991).

Management of CD-ROM Databases in ARL Libraries. (SPEC KIT 169) Washington, D.C.: Assn. of Research Libraries, 1990.

The New Papyrus: The Current and Future State of the Art. Ed. Steve Lambert and Suzanne Ropiequet. Redmond, Wash.: Microsoft Pr., 1986.

Nicholls, Paul T. *CD-ROM Collection Builder's Toolkit: The Definite Reference for CD-ROM Buyers.* Weston, Conn.: Eight Bit Books, 1991 (1992 edition).

Nissley, Meta. "CD-ROMs, Licenses and Librarians." In *CD-ROM Licensing and Copyright Issues for Libraries*, p.1–17. Ed. Meta Nissley and Nancy Melin Nelson. Westport, Conn.: Meckler, 1990.

Quint, Barbara. "Controversy over NLM CD-ROM Licensing Prices." *CD-ROM Librarian* 6, no. 4:24–26 (1991).

Rutherford, John. "Improving CD-ROM Management through Networking." *CD-ROM Professional* 3, no. 5:20–27 (1990).

Saffady, William. "CD-ROM: A Survey of Technology, Products, and Applications." *Library Computer Systems and Equipment* 12, no. 2:3–90 (1990).

Smith, Ian W. "Towards an Evaluation of CD-ROM Products in the Library User Services Environment." *Information Services and Use* 9:85–91 (1989).

Copyright and Licensing

"Copyright, CD-ROM, and Education." *TechTrends* 33, no. 3:38–39 (1988).

Duggan, Mary Kay. "Copyright of Electronic Information: Issues and Questions."

Online: The Magazine of Online Information Systems 15, no. 3:20–26 (1991).

Risher, Carol A. "Publishers, Librarians, and Copyright." *Library Acquisitions: Practice and Theory* 13, no. 3:213–16 (1989).

Talab, R. S. "Copyright and Other Legal Considerations in Patron-Use Software." *Library Trends* 40:85–96 (1991).

Tannenbaum, Jerry. "Database Licensing: Enhancing Access Cooperatively." *Wilson Library Bulletin* 65, no. 7:42–45 (1991).

General Works

The following are numbers in the Acquisitions Guidelines series, published by the Association for Library Collections and Technical Services, American Library Association.

Statistics for Managing Library Acquisitions. (Acquisitions Guidelines, no. 6) Chicago: ALA, 1989.

Guidelines for Handling Library Orders for In-Print Monographic Publications, 2nd ed. (Acquisitions Guidelines, no. 4) Chicago: ALA, 1984.

Guidelines for Handling Library Orders for Serials and Periodicals, rev. ed. (Acquisitions Guidelines, no. 7) Chicago: ALA, 1992.

Atkinson, Ross. "The Acquisitions Librarian as Change Agent in the Transition to the Electronic Library." *Library Resources & Technical Services* 36, no. 1:7–20 (1992).

Basch, Reva. "Books Online: Visions, Plans, and Perspectives for Electronic Text." *Online: The Magazine of Online Information Systems* 15, no. 4:13–23 (1991).

Demas, Sam. "Mainstreaming Electronic Formats." *Library Acquisitions: Practice and Theory* 13, no. 3:227–32 (1989).

Doherty, Richard M., and others. "Libraries and Computing Centers: Issues of Mutual Concerns." *Journal of Academic Librarianship* 13, no. 5:298a–98d (1987).

Downes, Robin N. "Electronic Technology and Access to Information." *Journal of Library Administration* 12, no. 3:51–62 (1990).

deKlerk, Ann. "Electronic Publishing and Networking 92." *C&RL News* 53, no. 3:181–82 (1992).

Hayes, Robert M. "A Summary of the Institute on Collection Development for the Electronic Library." *Library Acquisitions: Practice and Theory* 14:359–70 (1990).

Library Hi-Tech. Ann Arbor, Mich.: Pierian, 1983– .

Martin, Susan K. "Information Technology and Libraries: Toward the Year 2000." *College and Research Libraries* 50, no. 4:397–405 (1989).

Mason, Marylyn Gell. "Library Automation: The Next Wave." *Library Administration & Management* 5, no. 1:34–36 (1991).

Ohl Rice, Patricia. "From Acquisitions to Access." *Library Acquisitions: Practice and Theory* 14:15–21 (1990).

PC Software and Hardware Evaluation Newsletter. New York: Q-M Consulting Group, 1985–   .

Robinson, Barbara M. "Managing Change and Sending Signals in the Marketplace." *Library Acquisitions: Practice and Theory* 13, no. 3:217–26 (1989).

"A Study of the Review Literature for Electronic Technologies." *RQ* 32, no. 1:37–47 (1992).

Snyder, Fritz. "The Impact of New Technologies on Law Library Acquisitions." *Legal Reference Services Quarterly* 6, no. 3/4: 159–68 (1986).

Upham, Lois. "Library Automation in the Year 2000 A.D.," *Technical Services Quarterly* 1:73–78 (1983).

Glossaries and Dictionaries

Freedman, Alan. *The Computer Glossary: The Complete Illustrated Desk Reference*. 6th ed. New York: AMACOM, 1993.

Longley, Dennis, and Michael Shain. *MacMillan Dictionary of Information Technology*. 3rd ed. London: MacMillan, 1989.

Machovec, George S. *Telecommunications and Networking Glossary*. LITA Guides 3. Chicago: Library and Information Technology Association, ALA, 1990.

Miller, Rockley L., and others. *Videodisc and Related Technologies: A Glossary of Terms*. Falls Church, Va.: Future Systems Inc., 1988.

Local Area Networks (LANs)

Eddison, Elizabeth. "A LAN Toolbox." *Database* June 1989:15–21.

Flint, David C. "Selecting a Local Area Network for Personal Computers." *Netlink* 3, no. 1:4–8 (1987).

Germann, Christopher, Ed. "High-Performance Network Operating Systems." *LAN Times* 7, no. 4 (1990).

Learn, Larry L., ed. "This LAN Is My LAN, This LAN Is Your LAN (a Look at Linking LANs)." *Library High Tech News* 70:13–19 (1990).

Madron, Thomas W. *Local Area Networks: The Second Generation.* New York: Wiley, 1988.

Nasatir, M., and others. "Local Area Networks." *Information Technology and Libraries* 9, no. 1:89–108 (1990).

Rushineck, Avi. "Local Area Networks (LN) Case Study." *Resource Sharing and Information Networks* 4, no. 2:31–35 (1989).

Saffady, William. "Local Area Networks: A Survey of the Technology." *Library Technology Reports* 26, no. 1:5–125 (1990).

Strehlo, Christine. "How to talk LANSpeak." *Personal Computing* February 1989: 102–8.

Laserdiscs

Dick, Jeff T. "Laserdisc Redux." *Library Journal* 115, no. 20:36–39 (1990).

Hetch, Jeff. *The Laser Guidebook.* 2nd ed. New York: McGraw, 1992.

Kaatrude, Peter B. "Probing the Optical Disc Lease/Purchase Decision." *Proceedings of the Online, Inc. Conference, Chicago, 7–9 November 1989, 97–101.* Weston, Conn.:Online, Inc., 1990.

MacConnell, Karen. "Optical Technology: Interacting with Traditional Systems." *Wilson Library Bulletin* 61, no. 10:21–24 (1987).

Pratt, Douglas. *The Laser Video Disc Companion: A Guide to the Best (and the Worst) Laser Video Discs.* New York: Zoetrope, 1988.

Van Arsdale, William O. "The Rush to Optical Disks." *Library Journal* 111, no. 16: 53–55 (1986).

Preservation

Mallinson, John C. "On the Preservation of Human and Machine-Readable Records." *Information Technology and Libraries* 7, no. 1:19–23 (1988).

Saffady, William. "Stability, Care and Handling of Microforms, Magnetic Media, and Optical Disks." *Library Technology Reports* 27, no. 1:5–116 (1991).

Selection

Bullard, Scott R. "Collection Development in the Electronic Age: Selected Papers and Complementary Reports." *Library Acquisitions: Practice & Theory* 13, no. 3:209–12 (1989).

Dewey, P. R. "Looking at Review Sources." In *The Library Microcomputer Environment: Management Issues*, p.63–76. Ed. Sheila S. Intner and Jane Anne Hannigan. Phoenix: Oryx, 1988.

Guappone, Rebecca A., Beth J. Shapiro, and Scott R. Bullard. "Integrating Electronic Publishing into the Concepts and Practices of Collection Development." *Library Acquisitions: Practice and Theory* 14:327–39 (1990).

Herzog, Kate. "Collection Development for the Electronic Library." *Computers in Libraries* 10, no. 10:9–13 (1990).

Intner, Sheila S. "Selecting Software." *Library Acquisitions: Practice and Theory* 13, no. 3:233–40 (1989).

Machovec, George S. "Selection Criteria for Leasing Databases on CD-ROM and Magnetic Tape." *Online Libraries and Microcomputers* 6, no. 3:1–4 (1988).

Reed-Scott, Jutta. "Information Technologies and Collection Development." *Collection Building* 9, no. 3/4:47–51 (1989).

Seiden, Peggy. "Selection of Software for Patron Use in Libraries." *Library Trends* 40, no. 1:6–41 (1991).

Software
Brady, Mary Louise, Ilene F. Rockman, and David B. Walch. "Software for Patron Use in Libraries: Physical Access." *Library Trends* 40, no. 1:63–84 (1991).

Database. Weston, Conn.: Online, Inc. 1978– .

Library Software Review: SR. Westport, Conn.: Meckler, 1984– .

Microcomputer Software Policies in ARL Libraries. (SPEC KIT 123) Washington, D.C.: Assn. of Research Libraries, 1986.

Ogburn, Joyce, and Kim N. Fisher. "Acquiring Software for the Academic Library: New Horizons for Acquisitions." *Collection Management* 13, no. 3:69–84 (1990).

Software Digest Macintosh Ratings Report. Philadelphia: National Software Testing Laboratories, 1988– .

Software Digest Ratings Reports. Philadelphia: National Software Testing Laboratories, 1987– .

The Software Encyclopedia. London, New York: Bowker, Saur, 1990.

Truett, Carol. *Microcomputer Software Sources: A Guide for Buyers, Librarians, Programmers, Business People, and Educators*. Englewood, Colo.: Libraries Unlimited, 1990.

Index